AF709296

We Met at Starbucks

A Love Story

Eric L. Mott and Kelly Jo Eldredge

PublishAmerica
Baltimore

© 2008 by Eric L. Mott and Kelly Jo Eldredge.
All rights reserved. No part of this book may be reproduced, stored in a retrieval system or transmitted in any form or by any means without the prior written permission of the publishers, except by a reviewer who may quote brief passages in a review to be printed in a newspaper, magazine or journal.

First printing

ISBN: 1-60563-163-9
PUBLISHED BY PUBLISHAMERICA, LLLP
www.publishamerica.com
Baltimore

Printed in the United States of America

Dedication

We would like to dedicate this book to our parents, Gary and Carolyn Mott, and Cliff and Janis Eldredge, for providing such wonderful examples of love and partnership—eighty-six combined years of marriage and counting! Thank you for trusting us, accepting us, and teaching us to go for broke when it comes to love.

Most of all, thanks for remaining calm when we announced our engagement after only three weeks of dating!

Foreword

Whenever we tell people the story about how we met, they usually respond, "Oh, you should write a book."

Okay.

Chapter 1
Introduction

"Where did you two meet?"

Most people who learn we are getting married ask this question, along with other common queries like the following: When is the wedding? How long have you known each other? How do the four cats get along? You don't really have two white Jeeps, do you?

These questions, asked by both friends and strangers, indicate polite curiosity about our romance. That's life—romance interests people. For some reason, though, that first one is hard to answer. Almost every time someone asks us where we met, we turn to each other, smile, and laugh awkwardly. We lock eyes with a panicky feeling of indecision that says, "How are we going to answer this time?"

The truth is we met online, using the web-based dating service. There is no shame in that, for many people meet this way in today's society. However, our love runs so deep, and our relationship is so rich and rewarding, that we feel we were custom-made for each other. The idea that we met using a contrived method like online dating feels anti-climactic to us; it should be more profound than that. We first met in person at a Starbucks, but that's not even half the story.

We stammer and return our gazes to the questioner who, by now, invariably believes there must be some astonishing narrative behind the answer. We feel slightly embarrassed that there is not, and stammer some more. Then, we respond in unison, "We met at Starbucks!"

"Wow," the questioner typically responds, in a deep and thoughtful tone. "You mean you just randomly met at a coffee shop?"

"YES! That's *exactly* how it happened."

We met at Starbucks. It was latte at first sight.

Chapter 2
Returning Home: He Said…

My house looked familiar and foreign at the same time. I had let myself in hours, perhaps even minutes, after my soon-to-be ex-wife drove away in her U-Haul, traveling east. After three months of exile, I felt conflicting emotions of triumph and trepidation about moving back into the home we had shared together for seven years.

I walked around the quiet house to take a mental inventory of its contents. Some rooms looked exactly as I remembered them with furniture and decorations left untouched. Other rooms were completely empty and devoid of furnishings. I remembered the day we sat around the dining room table with a yellow notepad and made the list of "her" stuff and "my" stuff—the same dining room table that was by then traveling hundreds of miles east on I-70 at sixty-five miles per hour.

Everything seemed to be in order in the kitchen, and then I saw it: our wedding unity candle left on top of a cabinet where it had sat on display for years. My heart quaked and my stomach deflated. *Why would she leave that?* I thought to myself. *On the other hand, why would she want it?* The hope for love in marriage it represented no longer existed, replaced instead by the disappointment of two people who had grown irreconcilably apart.

I grabbed the candle with trembling hands to impulsively throw it away, but the waste can under the sink was missing—probably also traveling east on I-70—so instead I placed the white cylinder gingerly on the countertop. After examining it for several minutes, I lifted it again and stripped the ribbons, beads, and the placard of sentimental words off the wax. They came off easily, and the candle was then just another candle, devoid of symbolism but still useful. It would burn brightly in my living room for many months to come.

I visited the master bedroom last, and it was completely bare.

My feelings during the divorce process remained neutral, and I could not shed a tear during those months of separation. However, seeing that empty bedroom gave me a kicked-in-the-stomach feeling as badly as seeing the unity candle. I sat on the floor of that empty bedroom and cried for the first time. "What am I going to do, now?" I asked myself repeatedly.

As I sat there on the floor hugging myself with a hollow, empty feeling of mourning deep in my gut, one of my cats entered the room. Kyle, an empathetic, overweight grey tabby, walked into the room and sat several feet away from me. The cats! Where had they been? Probably sleeping the afternoon away in the basement. (I got the house and the cats; she took her dog and the retirement fund.)

Kyle is famous for just sitting and watching you with a blank, expressionless stare. "Hello! Where is Maggie?" I asked Kyle as he sat and watched me from a short distance. In response, he flopped onto the floor and rolled over onto his back with what sounded to me like a sigh of relief, as if to say, "The big, scary dog finally left!" He continued to look at me with a blank expression and examined me carefully—upside down—like he was thinking, *Who are you, by the way?*

(I found Maggie later that evening, a shy female who hid in the basement for several days, perhaps waiting to convince herself the big, scary dog was never coming back.)

I survived that day, and the days to follow. That first day returning home was the only time I felt uncomfortable in that house. I made a new life there myself with the help of a live-in roommate, the two cats—and some cool new bachelor furniture.

Life was good.

Chapter 3
Leaving Home: She Said…

I unlocked the series of deadbolts to our Washington Heights apartment, feeling like a thief entering the home that was no longer mine. My soon-to-be-ex-husband had agreed to vacate the premises for several hours while I retrieved my last few personal items. Most of the things we deemed to be "mine" when we divvied up our lives a few weeks previously were halfway to Colorado and my parents' basement.

I would be subletting a room in a fellow actor's apartment for the summer and then back on the road with a new tour in the fall. Basically, I was homeless.

"Hello?" I called out as I tiptoed into the apartment. No answer. I glanced around the living room, taking note of the rearrangement of his half of the furniture. My items had been boxed up and neatly left in plain sight. However, I passed them by and took one more walk through what was supposed to be our dream apartment in New York City. Spot—his cat now—stared at me accusingly from the sofa.

Guilt and remorse squeezed my heart as I toured the apartment: cluttered shelves of music; the large, white desk we had made out of a door; the bass viol propped up in the corner; the slim hallway of a kitchen—spacious by New York standards; the tiny bathroom we had planned several times to remodel but never did. Suddenly, I was hit square in the face by the fact that there was no more "we." How long would it take me to stop referring to myself in the plural?

I could no longer invade his home. I raced back down the long, creaky, wooden hallway, picked up my box, and flew out the door, stopping only to carefully lock all deadbolts.

Tears leaked unceasingly from the corners of my eyes as I took the ancient elevator to the first floor and escaped into the warm summer air. I hid my face from the doorman, who was confused by my evasive response to his chipper wave. Every step I took toward the A Train was a mixture of relief and regret, a painful shedding of my previous life.

On the long subway ride to my temporary room in Queens, I rested my aching head against the box on my lap. Now I was grieving, but transformation was coming. A glimmer of hope churned in my belly. Monumental changes were at that moment shaking my life apart. I had no idea how they were laying the groundwork for a future I could never have imagined.

Chapter 4
The Rule of Starbucks Proximity: He Said…

My first reaction to divorce was one of mild panic to finding myself single again—amazing how one's self-worth takes a hit when you can no longer use the pronoun "we." Before my divorce even became final I began worrying about how I would meet someone else.

I later would become comfortable in my own skin as a single man, but in the early days I felt confused. I had to learn how to be divorced first, before I could start dating again, but I didn't know that yet. Some lessons in life come the hard way.

"How do singles meet these days?" I asked myself.

Church felt like a good answer at first. However, a thirty-something single person seemed like a rare demographic group in my congregation. Maybe if I actually had attended with any regularity I would have increased my chances there.

"Hi! Praise God from whom all blessings flow! Want to go to the movies after worship?"

I was taking martial arts lessons at the time of my divorce. Maybe that would work? No. I couldn't see myself knocking some sweaty woman in an oversized, white canvas gi on her ass, offering her a hand up, and then asking her out on a date.

Where else could I go to meet people? Dance clubs? I don't dance. Plus, you can't hear yourself think in those places, let alone have a conversation.
"HI, YOU ARE CUTE. YOU WANNA GO OUT ON A DATE?"

"WHAT?"

I've heard that bars are good places to pick people up. I know all the right things to say: "Hi there. You come here often?" No thanks!

Would the grocery store work? Maybe. I like to cook, so I make frequent trips there. I thought I could stand in the produce aisle and look confused and helpless. Some compassionate woman would surely notice my plight and give assistance. I saw an attractive, helpful woman in a grocery store once, except my roommate was with me at the time. He and I were debating the difference between scallops, shallots, and scallions. The woman looked at us funny and said "green onions" as she walked by.

I heard many radio ads for Internet dating services during the fall of 2002. This was a brave new dating world—looking for love on the World Wide Web, from the anonymous privacy of your own home. I could do that!

I thought I was such an innovator in those days, as if I was the first person to discover this concept. I asked another divorced man at my office if he had ever used online dating. He said, yes, he had been using it for quite some time. Rats, I wasn't the first one, after all. He told me it worked great, and that he never had a lack of prospects each weekend. He was a player, though. Would it work for me?

Still only just separated and living in my sister's basement, I signed myself up and created my first online profile: hello, *elm741*! Several emails immediately inundated me, and I thought I had found a gold mine. Unfortunately, they were all notes from hopeful women outside the United States, presumably looking for a quick way to enter the country. I'm pretty sure St. Petersburg is not within fifty miles of zip code 80130.

I'm embarrassed by how naive I was in those early days. The first time I struck up a serious email conversation with someone online, I thought I was home free. *Phew,* I thought*, that was easy. Someone likes me!* Five years later, however, I was still looking. Reality check!

I smile to recall just how much time and effort I invested on the online dating process. Thousands of emails and "winks" were sent; hundreds of hours were spent perusing the online profiles of single women in greater Denver. Now that I have met Kelly, I am so relieved I stayed with it, because clearly the effort was worthwhile.

As the knowledge of how much work this was going to be sunk in, I calmed down and settled into the pattern of online dating. It usually went something like this:

Search the online postings for hours each day. Contact women you find attractive, and respond to women when they contact you. Email furiously for several days with someone of potential mutual interest, then go on a first date.

Go out on a second date with that person and burn bridges with everyone else you have been communicating with to that point. Then, break up with the person by date number three. Start the cycle all over again—search online postings for hours each day…

Where to meet someone for that first date was always an interesting question. I've met people in restaurants, bars, arcades, malls, Whole Foods stores, homes, coffee shops, sporting events, concerts, and street corners.

By far the easiest and most convenient place to meet someone on a first date is Starbucks. The atmosphere is neutral and low-key; you don't have to worry about loud music, bar tabs, or who pays the restaurant bill. I always felt most comfortable at a coffee shop, and besides, Starbucks are everywhere. I discovered that if I drew a straight line between my house and my date's house, that line would pass within a quarter mile of a Starbucks halfway between us.

That's my Rule of Starbucks Proximity.

I developed a reputation at the office for being a player during this time. It was embarrassing and slightly alarming, because that is not my style. That's the nature of the online dating world, though.

Introductions were too numerous to count, and they made Monday morning team meetings interesting.

"Still going out with so-and-so, Eric?"

"Nope, I've gone out with a few since that one!"

"Oh? How many women did you meet this weekend?"

"Three."

Eric searches the faces of his co-workers seated around the table and sees slack-jawed, wide-eyed expressions everywhere. Eric sinks slowly in his chair and hopes the meeting starts soon.

Chapter 5
Oh, Great: She Said…

I am sitting in a room that smells like sweat and stale coffee. I don't want to be here, but I'm glued to my chair. I'm surrounded by about seventy-five jolly people I don't know and don't really care to get to know. The hairs on my arms are standing on end, probably because it is 115 degrees outside and about forty-five degrees in this room. An ancient air conditioner noisily blows waves of frigid air across the crowd.

I'm tired, I'm irritable, I'm fidgety, I want to crawl out of my skin, and—oh, great. It's my turn.

"Hi, I'm Kelly, and I'm an alcoholic. I have thirty days of sobriety today."

The crowd goes wild.

I shuffle up to the podium and receive a shiny token of my achievement and a bear hug from an overweight, over-excited woman who whispers in my ear, "It's going to be okay. Don't leave before the miracle happens!"

What miracle?

"Keep comin' back!" an anonymous male voice yells from the back of the room.

"I'll be sure to do that," I mutter and return to my seat.

After the meeting, a friendly woman in a smart-looking business suit and heels I would have great difficulty attempting to walk in glides across the room and approaches me with a broad smile.

"Hey, Kelly. I wanted to tell you about an awesome ladies meeting on Tuesdays at five-thirty. Here's the info. You should check it out. The men may try to grab your ass, but the women will save it! Trust me."

I have no idea what she is talking about, but I take the paper.

My mind sputters, *Nobody better even try to grab my ass in here.* I stare suspiciously at an unsuspecting man walking by with two cups of coffee for himself and a friend. *I'll slug the fool who even attempts…freaky, happy ex-drunks. I'm tired of being grumpy. I find it hard to believe none of these people drink, because they are way too happy to be here.*

I wander out into the blazing sunlight and search the parking lot for my mom. She is nowhere in sight. That means I will have to endure another five minutes of small talk with these crazies. Oh, great.

A lot has changed since I left New York City a few years ago. I reached the height of my performing career and the depths of my personal life, and I landed here…in hell. Well, it seems like hell. It's a billion degrees outside, and I'm living with my parents.

I shove the slip of paper in my pocket and cross my arms, glaring out across the parking lot and building a serious resentment against my mother. I have no idea that little piece of paper will be my ticket to an entirely new way of life.

I don't know why I did it, but I went to that Tuesday meeting. It was there that I met a new group of friends I came to love and trust, and I started a healing process that would transform me.

I didn't know on that hot, sticky day that I was starting to change. There was a tiny kernel of hope within me that glowed a brilliant sapphire blue, even through the darkness I had created.

I would be happy again.

I would get myself back.

I just didn't know it yet.

Chapter 6
9/11: He Said…

I took Kelly to the cemetery on a September afternoon. It's one of my favorite places.

Brightly colored pinwheels spun eagerly in the breeze, clicking and fluttering with soothing sounds that mingled with the tinkling of multitudes of sun catchers and small chimes. We saw the foothills of the Colorado Rockies rise thirty miles to the west. Their purple shapes rose and fell in jagged lines along the horizon. A marble statue of Jesus playing with children sat nearby.

Everywhere we saw flowers, stuffed animals, and toys. Why would we find such joyful, colorful things in a cemetery? We were standing in a special garden called "Babyland"—my daughter rests here.

I felt honored that Kelly would accompany me to this sacred place to view the grave of my daughter born to a woman from my past—a woman she does not know and will never meet.

The memories came back to me as echoes and shadows softened and dimmed by the passage of time. Could it have been seven years already?

I remembered the ultrasound techs and doctors huddled in conference and whispering together with nervous glances. I remembered the confusing, panicked trip to the hospital in the ambulance, the ominous silence of the heart monitor, and the painful, risky delivery of an infant that did not cry, nor ever would. Then, the pastor sprinkled water on the child's head and held her high into the air, as if introducing her to God. The truth is he already knew her and welcomed her home.

I remembered holding my lifeless daughter, wrapped in towels, at arm's length. I was confused and afraid, wondering what her skin felt like but too terrified to touch it. I never touched my daughter, and I have to live with that for the rest of my life. I remember leaving the hospital in a car that felt empty with two people when there should have been three—the promise of a child denied.

Numb, dazed phone calls followed to family, friends, and the funeral home. Because of the circumstances, I had to plan the memorial service myself. I sat in that funeral home alone. I sat there, lonelier that I had ever felt before, and chose my daughter's grave marker and planned her memorial. I did the best I could.

I remembered how small the casket was—almost as small as a shoebox. I remembered my father after the funeral service, bent over double, his body wracked with sobs, consumed by the anguish that I felt but was too numb to display. I carried that casket from the chapel cradled in my arms, all eyes on me—alone, isolated. You do not need pallbearers for an infant.

I shared those memories with Kelly as we stood there in that place on that September afternoon. They were important memories, a part of my past she needed to know to understand who I was and where I had been.

Then, I knelt by the grave marker and flicked stray weeds and blades of grass off the stone. I leaned down and kissed the cold marble. Then I stood, took Kelly's hand, and we walked back to the car; I felt content.

The cemetery is one of my favorite places; 9/11 is a day of remembrance to me, but not for the same reasons as the rest of the world. My daughter was stillborn on September 11, 2000.

The mourning is over; the pain is gone. Now I have memories. I feel happy and peaceful when I visit the cemetery—a favorite, sacred place. I am a father. I have a daughter, and she knows me.

Someday, I will know her.

Chapter 7
With Friends Like That: She Said…

Returning to the dating scene after being married for ten years is…well, it's an experiment. It was a continual work in progress for me. After my first online conversation, I realized that I had a lot to learn, and my education continued until the point I looked into Eric's eyes.

The evening I sat down in my newly purchased condo in Scottsdale to fill out my Internet dating profile, I joyfully joined the experiment. I found out quickly that there are unwritten rules, there are preconceived notions, and there are lots of expectations that come with online dating. I also found out that none of those things had to apply to me.

One of the unwritten rules I actually enjoyed was: *A first date should take place at Starbucks.*

I am intimately familiar with the layout of just about every Starbucks in the metro Phoenix and metro Denver areas by now, and I can say without a doubt that Starbucks is a safe first date location. If there was a spark of interest, we could sit there for hours getting to know each other. If not, the date was as quick and painless as downing a cup of espresso.

A couple of my close friends teased me mercilessly about my new explorations in dating. They claimed to be amazed at how I would jump back into the fray, even after what seemed to be a never-ending series of disappointments. So, they decided to help me out a little. They tried numerous tactics to get me to divulge the Starbucks location of my upcoming first dates, because they felt they could do me the invaluable service of screening my prospects.

Yep, my buddies wanted to plant themselves behind a book or newspaper in the popular coffeehouse. Then, when my date wasn't looking, they intended to hold up cards that would rate him from one to ten. They fancied themselves Olympic judges or something. I don't know.

I did *not* ever divulge the location of my first dates. I did, however, call one of my girlfriends before and after each date. That was our compromise. They would know I was safe; I wouldn't have to explain their shenanigans to some guy whom I barely knew; my date would not end up in therapy.

Unfortunately, I eventually let my girlfriends meet several romantic interests who made it past the Starbucks Test.

Here is a typical example of how one of those meetings went: I was singing a solo one Sunday in church and planned to go to lunch with everyone afterward. The poor, unsuspecting gentleman had not yet met the girls. He did have the unfortunate luck to sit in the pew directly in front of them when he arrived a few minutes before the service began.

One of the gang realized within seconds that he was the guy and decided to have a little fun. She leaned over and not-so-quietly whispered to friend #2, "So, Kelly's new flame is supposed to be here. Is this the guy she's dating, or is it the guy she's sleeping with?"

With friends like that…

Actually, in all seriousness, my friends and family were invaluable to me as I forged through the dating world. In the early days of my dating they thought more highly of me than I did of myself, and they encouraged me to raise my standards. Friends and family members have taught me that I'm a pretty great catch; that I sometimes have rotten judgment when it comes to choosing a man; that I need a guy who can be a little goofy and not always take himself seriously; that chemistry matters; that it might be a good idea to have at least one or two similar interests; that I'm not perfect, and neither is he; that I deserve to have my dreams come true.

I never would have met Eric if it hadn't been for the insight and encouragement of these people. They told me to go for broke and not settle. They also brought out the best in me. They taught me that in order to be a good date, I needed to be comfortable in my own skin and perfectly happy on my own first. They also exhibited terrific examples of love and commitment in their own relationships—particularly my parents. I wanted what they had.

I discovered myself during these experiments, and as wonderful, funny, strange, sad, or disturbing as some of them were, each one helped me to get to the truth about what I want out of life and what I can give to a relationship.

I feel that I grew into my skin during those experimental years. Sometimes I wish I had met Eric a long time ago, but I know deep in my heart I met him at the perfect time.

Chapter 8
My Quest for Authenticity: He Said…

Creating an interesting narrative for my online profile was challenging for me. I took great pains to ensure that my honest personality came through in the words I used in the website's narrative portion to describe myself. If I bragged about my life too much, someone I really liked would eventually call me on it. I decided to be up-front from the beginning. I am a modest, low-key person by nature, so I felt I was always at a disadvantage compared to the bolder men of the world, but I was willing to take that chance. Someone out there would surely appreciate my honesty!

Beyond online matchmaking and my cyber-self, my life experienced some gratifying transformations during this period. In order for my true personality to show in my online words, I needed to know what that personality was. I realized that if I wanted to avoid the same mistakes that led to my divorce, my way of thinking needed to change. The old model evidently did not work, so I needed a new one. Some people might call this finding or reinventing yourself. I prefer to call it my "quest for authenticity."

I always felt I had a healthy understanding of my strengths, weaknesses, and potential. My main problem was that I was not reaching that potential; to me this represented my major mistake in my failed marriage. I was too passive in life and did not participate enough in the world at large—a boring way to live.

What could I do to reach my potential as a vital, interesting person?

Everybody who lives in Colorado needs to learn to ski, right? Well then, I should learn, too. Luckily, I had a good friend who took me under his wing and tutored me at Breckenridge Ski Resort. I took to the slopes like a natural; by the end of my first day, I was whooshing down blue runs with gusto.

Lucky for me, Breckenridge has a nice, well-equipped emergency room right at the bottom of the mountain. The helpful ski patrol members will happily deliver you straight to the back door in their little red sleds pulled by snowmobiles. My separated shoulder healed quite nicely, but that was my one and only ski adventure that first year. I needed something else.

What else could I do to live life to the fullest?

I felt strongly that to avoid becoming one-dimensional by obsessing about dating and meeting women, I had to focus on something outside of myself, something that would benefit society. Thus began my journey in volunteerism. Admittedly, though, it took a long time to fulfill that plan. Finding inspiration was difficult, but finally I made my choice—I would volunteer for hospice.

I cannot explain the attraction I had for hospice, other than to say it was probably as far out of my comfort zone as I could possibly get. Maybe that was reason enough. I now think that affording someone with a terminal illness all the dignity, comfort, and fellowship we can give them is one of the most humane things we can do for a fellow person.

I met some fascinating people in my time with hospice. I get choked up when I consider the fact that they are all at peace now, but I feel so honored to have known them in the most sacred time in their journeys. I no longer volunteer for hospice, but I count experiences gained there as some of the most valuable in my life.

The knowledge I learned in a hiking club inspired me to volunteer for a local search-and-rescue team. I'm not sure why I thought a few hiking classes qualified me to go looking for people in the wilderness, but why not? It was a great excuse to purchase more equipment, a larger backpack, and a Jeep. Search-and-rescue is now my current focus for volunteerism. The learning curve has been, and will continue to be, huge for me, but the challenge is part of the fun, and I hope my teammates are glad to see me when the pager goes off. If only I could remember how to tie a butterfly knot in a rope!

Participating in life by trying new recreational activities or volunteering helped me get in touch with my authentic self. Another decision I made that helped me was the decision to do the things I enjoy, whether I had a date to share them with or not. I refused to stay home moping and went to the movies or to restaurants by myself countless times. I admit I had some self-consciousness to overcome at first, but I was proud to do it in the end.

I had a real weakness for Friday nights, however. It seemed like I could think of nothing better to do than go home after work and browse listings on the dating websites. There was a feature you can utilize that shows you profiles of people who are "online now," currently logged into the system. I was always curious who was home alone on a Friday night looking for love on their computer. Ah, Eric—that would be YOU.

Another tradition I started was to pamper myself each birthday. My favorite thing to do around my birthday in March was to spend a weekend in Glenwood Springs. After a day of skiing at Sunlight Resort, I would get a massage at the Yampah Spa and soak in the hot springs pool under the stars. I never really intended to go alone each year, but as it turns out, I never seemed to be dating anyone during the month of March. Go figure.

I did not lament the fact that I did so many activities alone. On the contrary, I felt those activities represented a celebration of self, and helped me in my quest for authenticity: saying what I wanted do and doing what I said I would, regardless. That's my definition of authenticity.

The calendar says December as I write this, Christmas mere days away. I remember last Christmas, before I met Kelly. I went snowshoeing by myself in the high country. A picture of Mt. Sniktau I snapped that day hangs in our office. I have to say that was one of the best Christmases I've ever had—the snow, the mountains, and the solitude made the day sacred. I'm proud to say I had a good Christmas alone on a holiday that celebrates family and togetherness. I have a feeling this Christmas will be just as good, if not better.

I did not save any of the profile narratives I wrote about myself. I wish I could go back in time and read them again to see how honest about myself I really was. Once Kelly agreed to marry me, I deleted my online profile and erased all copies of it from my computer. That was cathartic for me—one chapter closed, and a new one beginning.

I think I did all right.

Chapter 9
It Took Twelve Steps: She Said…

When I first walked into the rooms of AA, I thought my life was over. I knew I was an alcoholic. I never questioned that. But, I thought I was coming to a dead-end in my life. I was sick and tired of being sick and tired. I eventually learned that I was just venturing onto a new road that would literally save my life and take me to places I only previously dreamed of going.

I did not really try alcohol until I went to college, but I knew from the first time I took a drink that my reaction was not normal. One glass of wine set up a craving in me that I just couldn't seem to satisfy. I immediately hid my disease in a dark cloak of shame and guilt and carried it around with me everywhere I went, until my parents—God bless them—gave me the courage to admit the truth when I was visiting them in Arizona. It was my mom who called Alcoholics Anonymous to find local meetings. I was too sick, too scared, too humiliated. Her quiet strength showed me the way.

As I said, I thought my life was over at age thirty-six. I thought I had truly hit bottom. I couldn't imagine a life without alcohol, and I was quickly realizing that I wasn't holding on to much of a life with it. So, I gave up. I turned in the towel. I went to AA.

I remember telling my brother I was an alcoholic. I was so embarrassed, even though I was stating a fact that had probably been obvious to him for years. His response made me laugh and cry at the same time. He said, "Kelly, I'm your brother. I love you no matter what. I'm here for you—no matter what. Got it? I'd come and get you out of a gutter if I had to—of course there would be no big hugs—not until you cleaned up, anyway."

As uncomfortable as those first AA meetings were, I knew I had come home. Every person there was speaking my language, whether they were a professional businesswoman in a suit and high heels or a toothless homeless man who smelled like he hadn't bathed in a week. Alcoholism doesn't discriminate. I learned some of the most poignant and eloquent lessons on life and happiness and how to live daily in recovery from people who might have scared me if I met them in a dark alley.

I thought a future without alcohol was ominous, but they told me in the rooms of Alcoholics Anonymous to take it one day at a time, keep coming back, find a sponsor, and work the twelve steps.

By some miracle, that's what I ended up doing. I didn't do it perfectly by any stretch of the imagination. I learned a lot of lessons by making mistakes. I relapsed several times while trying to test my alcoholism. Finally, I admitted I was powerless. I took that first step.

I ended up moving to Arizona permanently and did a lot of work on my addiction before I ever signed up for Internet dating. To anyone who is struggling, I want to tell you that in my experience, there is an answer. You are not alone. It's not impossible. Life is by no means over. There is hope.

We all have something we struggle to overcome. For me, it was a pretty obvious thing. It's not my flaws that define me; it's how I overcome them.

Through AA I learned not only how not to drink, but how to be a better person. I learned that it is important to care for others and give back a little of what has been given to me. There were numerous Friday nights when I sat rolling my eyes in my sponsor's car as we traveled to a maximum security prison to volunteer by leading AA meetings behind bars. NOT what I preferred to be doing on a Friday night. But on the way home, my heart was full of gratitude, and I realized that giving back to my community is not just a good thing to do. It feels great! It was exactly where I needed to be on Friday nights in early recovery.

My first experiment in the dating world as a sober woman was rocky. It was almost exactly a year into my sobriety. (My sponsor strongly discouraged dating before my first anniversary date.)

When I think about the gentleman, we were not really compatible at all, but he was nice and friendly, and we laughed a lot as we got to know each other. On our second date, I blurted out that I was an alcoholic. I was terrified of what to say if he offered me a drink, even though I had been coached by several friends in AA who had been through the scenario before. I forgot everything they said and decided clumsily, and on the spur of the moment, to wipe out the chance that he might offer me a drink by telling him the truth first. For some inexplicable reason, I thought it would be better to beat him to the punch. At the time, he seemed to take the news in stride.

It took me three or four dates to know for sure that we were not a match. Unfortunately, he did not agree with me. This led me to my next dilemma—how to back out gracefully. Of course, I botched that one pretty badly, too, stumbling over my words and seeming very unsure of my decision, because I was trying so hard not to hurt his feelings. I was also a little nervous, because the guy knew a very big secret about me, and he was mad at me for breaking up with him. Could he cause any harm?

Well, he tried.

He fired off a bunch of angry emails and dropped off notes at my door that made him seem more like a stalker than someone who had gone out on a couple of dates with a woman he barely knew. His final email featured how he was thrilled to no longer be dating an alcoholic, because he was planning a trip to the mountains with a few friends, and they would be drinking expensive wine all weekend. He proceeded to go into great detail about how delicious and soothing the wine would taste, and how he couldn't wait to get a good buzz on. That was when I blocked his emails and phone calls.

I learned something very important from Experiment #1: I have nothing of which to be ashamed. I get to say I'm not interested in a guy when I'm not. I learned from that first step into dating that I am in charge of my future, and I don't have to stay with someone just because *they* think I should. That sounds kind of funny, but I had a lot to learn about boundaries. It was my first shaky step into discovering my own identity.

I'm proud to be an alcoholic in recovery. I understand now why anonymity is important until you get to know and trust someone, and I discovered that it was a good idea to wait a little longer before letting the next date in on my big secret. I was glad that I dealt with it head-on in Experiment #1, because it showed me that I was strong and healthy, and no guy would talk me into compromising my sobriety. Experiment #1 was a huge victory, but I had to take twelve steps first.

Chapter 10
Things People Say: He Said…

Keeping my sense of humor was vital for my survival in the online dating world. You have to have confidence in yourself, have a thick skin, and keep picking yourself up off the floor.

It also helps to be open-minded and honest about your own character. I always felt women could spot a fraud a mile away, so I was very careful about how I presented myself. I do admit I played games with my online profile from time to time. I was constantly re-working it, perhaps playing up strengths that I perceived I had from feedback from women I dated.

I also dropped and recreated my profile twice. I transitioned from *elm741*, which I thought was an uninspired nickname, to *rivercitynative*, a reference to my home town. Finally, I ended up as *kylethecat*, which is the name I used when Kelly first contacted me. Kyle is one of my cats. I thought maybe he could screen all the women for me and let me know whom he liked. Silly.

I don't really know why I thought making new profiles would help me. They were the same pictures after all, and probably mostly the same words. I know I wasn't fooling anybody. Besides, each time I created a new profile, I got all those emails from women outside the country. I'm pretty sure Beijing is not within fifty miles of zip code 80130.

Most women claim they want to meet a "nice guy," which I believe myself to be. However, it doesn't always work out that way. I've noticed that some women don't really know what they want until you give them what they ask for. For example, here are some flattering things I heard from women right before they broke up with me:

"You're perfect."

"It doesn't get any better than this."

"Aren't you quite the find?"

"Do you want to go to Vegas together?"

"I saw you online and created my account just to meet you!"

The penguins utter one of my favorite lines from the movie *Madagascar*, when one of them wonders if they should tell the animals departing the island that their boat is out of fuel. The penguin leader tells his companions to "Just smile and wave, boys!" That is what I began doing when I heard overly flattering phrases like that coming from my dates. "Smile and wave, Eric, just smile and wave!"

However, there are certain phrases I heard from women that would cause me to smile and *run*. In other words, here are some examples of phrases I heard right before *I* broke up with someone:

"I'm filing for bankruptcy next week."

"Who actually likes their parents, I mean really?"

"This could be a deal breaker…" (It usually was.)

"I think my kids would be more comfortable living at your house."

"I'd just as soon do it with a woman as with a man."

"I think that you think you need some space away from me."

"Do you want to go out with my sister?" followed closely thereafter by, "How dare you make a move on my sister!"

"I need to leave the country for three months."

"My friends really like you; I hate doing what my friends think is right."

I also noticed a correlation between things I did to impress someone and the probability that a relationship would end in the near future. Sometimes they were embarrassing, sometimes painful, and usually very expensive.

For example, I treated one woman to a romantic, Colorado getaway weekend and happily financed the entire trip. That was the last time I saw her, and little did I know just how expensive that trip would become.

Even my trusty Honda automobile made sacrifices for the dating scene, for that particular trip also coincided with the time I ruined my engine due to a mysterious lack of motor oil. The fact that it made a 300-mile journey up and over the Continental Divide and back with only half of a quart of oil gives testimony to Honda's toughness but held little financial consolation for me. Hint: Do not drive a vehicle that refuses to operate above 3,000 engine RPM.

I also took a trip to Las Vegas with someone I was dating seriously. Thankfully, we shared the expense of that trip fifty-fifty, but it was expensive, nonetheless. I believe that was the last time I saw her, too.

Another woman of interest was heavily involved as a volunteer in a national self-help organization. I attended a presentation she gave at her home—to impress her, of course—and eagerly plunked down $500 to attend one of their introductory weekend sessions. The group's message did not speak to me, so I skipped the Sunday session to salvage the rest of the weekend and earned a gruff call from one of the organization officials. "You must be in denial about something," he said. "Thanks for the five hundred dollars." You're welcome.

Nope, never saw her again.

I was an enthusiastic, if not talented, amateur runner in those days. I once ran a local four-mile race in Denver with a woman I was dating. Her effortless, gliding running pace was hard for me to keep up with, but I was determined. I finished ahead of her, but my legs and feet hurt for a month and I gave up running for good after that. I never saw her again after the race.

I would not recommend inviting someone to be your guest at a wedding unless you are sure you are on solid ground with that person. I took someone to a wedding once, and our frosty relationship must have been noticeable, for my friends asked me if my guest and I were dating. I didn't actually know the answer to that, so I had to turn to the woman and confirm if we actually were, or not. She said yes, but I never saw her again, either.

Finally, I noticed a correlation over the years that seemed to indicate that the more I bragged about someone to my mother, the more likely a break-up with that person was imminent. Thus, when I met Kelly and realized immediately that we had potential, I was superstitiously tight-lipped with Mom.

Eric: "Hi Mom! I met someone new. She's okay."

One week later...

Eric: "Hi Dad. Kelly and I are engaged!"

Dad: "Who's Kelly?"

Chapter 11
Next! She Said…

One of my closest friends had a favorite saying whenever I appeared less than enthusiastic about a dating experience.

"NEXT!"

I liked her attitude.

Don't get depressed. Don't get mad. Don't worry about it. Consider what you learned from the experience, what you might do differently, and move on.

Let's just say I kissed a lot of frogs before I met Eric, and it was worth every slimy smooch.

Experiment #3: Date with tall, dark, handsome MBA, originally from New York. He showed up in a Porsche and paid for lunch. Within minutes, I was stifling a yawn as he bored me with endless talk of his stock trades of the day, advice on how I should be investing my money, and continuous references to the number of times he had hiked Pinnacle Peak that week. He insulted Midwesterners at least three times, even though I told him I was originally from Iowa.

Experiment #4: Coffee date with tall, dark laser salesman and advocate for children's rights. We spent two hours at the coffee station at Barnes and Noble while he tearfully relayed the story of the death of his daughter at the hand of his drug-and-alcohol-addicted wife. (I chose not to take that moment to let him know I was in recovery.) The fact that he was "God's vessel" was mentioned no less than forty-five times. Further research after the date revealed he also boasted a colorful arrest record, including violating a restraining order and identity theft. He emailed me shortly after our date to tell me I wasn't his type. Whew.

Experiment #5: Starbucks date with tall, handsome, funny, father of two. We seemed to really hit it off and laughed a lot as we got to know each other over a cup of coffee. An hour and a half later we departed with a quick hug, and he asked if he could call me to schedule a second date. I was thrilled, and I went right home and emailed him a note to thank him for the coffee and tell him I was looking forward to our next date. However, days passed, and he never contacted me again. I must have completely misread the signs that he wasn't really interested.

Experiment #6: Phone date planned with tall, handsome former Midwestern farm boy, now bio-engineer, who was also in the process of getting his Ph.D. Successful first date at Starbucks led to plans for a second date, even though he was not nearly as tall as he claimed to be in his profile, and sometimes I had no idea what he was talking about when he went into engineer-speak.

Under favorite activities he listed "getting slightly lost."

Second date revealed that he recently decided to take apart a seven-foot grand piano in his living room. When I asked why, he couldn't come up with an answer. Second date fizzled somewhere between his living room and dinner, and there was no third.

Experiment #23: He didn't like coffee, so we couldn't have our first date at Starbucks. Instead, he suggested appetizers at a trendy restaurant in Tempe. He asked me within the first five minutes if I usually "glam up" more, or if I was just having an off day. (He assumed since I used to be an actress I would wear more makeup.) He didn't glam up for me, either, by the way. He was wearing a faded Hawaiian shirt and jeans, and I suspected he had not yet combed his hair that day.

In discussing his recent divorce, he asked, "What do *you* consider abuse?" I knew that wasn't a good sign, but I took the bait.

"Well, there are several types. Why? What happened?"

"Well, I told her that her butt was big. Do you think that's abuse?"

"I don't think it's nice."

"She took some feminist class, and then she thought she could do whatever she wanted."

"Uh…she can."

He obviously wasn't listening to me.

When I emailed him after the date to let him know that I didn't think we were a good match, he responded with, "Well, I guess I'll just have to find someone else to travel the world with."

Guess so.

Experiment #30: Independently wealthy musician. (I didn't think those two items could exist in the same sentence, but in this case, they did.) He said he didn't drink anymore after receiving a DUI, but judging from the liquor cart in his living room, I guessed he was not being entirely truthful.

He invited me to his symphony concert, and it was a very lovely evening until he nearly shoved me behind a parked car when we ran into his ex-fiancee (violinist) in the parking lot.

During the drive home, I nursed my twisted ankle from the parking lot incident while he told me a little more about his leanings toward depression. He claimed that I could not possibly understand his occasional depression, because I didn't know what it was like to play heart-wrenching music, and I knew nothing of the incredible amount of practice and discipline it required.

How could I possibly understand him? Never mind the fact that I had a graduate degree from New England Conservatory and spent numerous years as a paid professional musician in classical music, jazz, and musical theatre.

Not once have I found music to be depressing. It can be heart-wrenching, beautiful, sad, or joyful—never depressing. It's a gift to be a musician.

When I finally told him at the end of our second date that I didn't think it was working out, he said, "Well, that makes me very sad, and I think you should change your mind. I've decided that you're perfect for me. You're pretty and young, you understand music, and you have *almost* no flaws—except for the fact that you're an alcoholic."

Experiment #75: This one was a surprise. On the phone he sounded like Sean Penn's character in *Fast Times at Ridgemont High*. I thought to myself, *This guy must be a pothead,* as he lazily told me his life story. But when we met, he was very intelligent. He talked nonstop about the Discovery Channel and books he had read and his investments in real estate. I found out his accent came from several years of living in Hawaii. Still, he had a flower child side. I would bet $100 he had a lava lamp somewhere in his house. He never contacted me again after our first date. I must have made a less than radical impression, dude.

Experiment #76: A snow storm cancelled our first date—a new twist for me, as I had newly moved to Denver from Phoenix. We had a lot of fun flirting and sending witty emails back and forth leading up to our rescheduled first date a week later. According to his profile he was very tall, had lots of muscles, was very active, had two teenage daughters (danger, danger), hated cats (HEY!), loved Sponge Bob (uh-oh), and his favorite flavor of ice cream was—drum roll, please—vanilla (you've got to be kidding me).

We met with high expectations at ten in the morning at Starbucks. He was a skinny bald dude, barely taller than me. I was not sure where the muscles were hiding beneath his coat, but I was 99 percent sure he had 0 percent body fat.

I was uneasy with our strained face-to-face conversation and blurted out a joke about vanilla ice cream, which included a reference to my ex, who was also a big fan of the flavor. That set him off.

"Do NOT compare me to your ex-husband! I will NOT have that!"

Obviously, the witty banter had been left on the Internet. When I politely emailed a thank you, but the chemistry just wasn't there, he asked if I might be willing to have a physical relationship with no strings attached. Did I mention the lack of chemistry? Was he listening?

Experiment #78: I'm not exactly sure how we made it to a third date, but it was my worst Valentine's Day EVER. There were no flowers or heart-shaped boxes of chocolates in his hands when he arrived at my doorstep to pick me up, and he took great pains to avoid mentioning the fact that it was February 14th. I quickly hid the small present I picked out for him under a pillow on the couch, and my cats spent the rest of the evening attempting to unearth it while I batted them away.

We did not go out that evening. Instead, he collapsed on my couch, and I listened to a monologue that would have thrown Mickey Mouse into a deep depression. My date told me about how difficult it was to find a new job (laid off two years ago); how he was stuck in this town for at least the next ten years, because he had joint custody of his kids; how his ex-wife was a total bitch and lived to make his life hell; how God made alcohol for the single parent; and how I better NOT expect him to drive the hour from his house to mine all the time, because THAT wasn't going to happen....But he wasn't saying he never wanted to see me again.

He left at nine-thirty, and I ended up watching the Soap Network and eating my weight in chocolate (given to me for Valentine's Day by my parents—not him).

Here are the top ten things I've learned through experimentation:

Google the guy *before* the first date.
Money isn't everything.

There is no reason to be mean, even if he's a jerk to you.
Guys almost always lie about their height.
Don't jump to conclusions.
Don't dumb down just to make him feel better.
Be honest.
Don't assume he will call, even if he says "I'll give you a call."
Laughter is good.
If you would be embarrassed to introduce him to your parents, move on.

I don't regret a single one of those experiments. They showed me what was important to me, they taught me something about humility, and they eventually led me to my one true love.

Chapter 12
Not All Who Wander Are Lost: He Said…

Not everything I did for love turned out poorly. Some relationships caused self-enhancing changes in my life. I sincerely believe that I carried something positive away from each relationship, no matter how it ended or how long it lasted. Sometimes, though, I had to look hard to see the hidden benefit in the long string of failures; but for the most part, I believe it. I also believe that positive spin helped me stay more optimistic than I would have otherwise during the interminable onslaught of introductions and first dates.

One woman, in particular, introduced me to a local hiking club. This would open doors to many adventures for me. I would rate this as one of the most important events I experienced during my dating journey prior to meeting Kelly.

I used to think hiking meant grabbing a water bottle and driving to the nearest urban trailhead parking lot. I didn't even own a true backpack when I attended my first hiking trip as a guest of that dating interest. What I had was more like a school bag—a tiny thing that barely held a pair of spare socks and a candy bar. How embarrassing.

Never again! Now I carry thirty-five pounds of very, very important stuff in my backpack. How I got to that point illustrates the truth that in hiking, as in life and dating, not all who wander are lost.

The club I joined stresses hiker education to encourage safety and offers many classroom opportunities for that purpose. This was something new and exciting to me! The Colorado back country has an immeasurable number of breathtaking sights to see, but I quickly learned that just carrying a water bottle wasn't going to get me there or keep me safe once I arrived.

One of my first experiences with hiker education was trekking school, the basic, entry-level class. During this class I learned about the essential items you must carry with you to be safe in the wilderness. Materials such as water, food, and spare clothing I understood readily. Check! I could do that. Sunglasses, lip balm, and sunscreen made sense to me, too. Roger! Sun safety is good. Matches and fire starters seemed okay, too. I like to play with fire. Okay! A flashlight makes good sense. Could I carry that huge Mag Lite I had out in the garage?

Bivouac gear? What is a bivouac?

A bivouac is an unplanned overnight stay in the back country. Sure—that sounded like something worth preparing for. You never know.

One fascinating aspect of the physical world we live in is that magnetic north and true north do not point in exactly same direction. Do you think that matters to a hiker? Not unless one carries a compass. Oh, yeah—I required one of those, too.

I needed a bigger backpack.

That year in the hiking club taught me a lot: planning a hike, route finding, preparation, safe back country travel habits, situational awareness—all good stuff. We even learned some basic winter and avalanche safety tips, important for the Colorado high country.

One particularly interesting exercise involved gaining skills with an ice axe for winter travel. We students learned a technique called self-arrest, where essentially we would climb to the top of a mountain and throw ourselves off headfirst or feet first—whatever—and use the axe to halt our fall before reaching the bottom or experiencing bodily harm, whichever came first. That was fun.

From then on, I carried my backpack full of survival gear wherever I went—even in state parks near my home. For example, Roxborough State Park is a jewel of a place south of Denver. Impossibly intricate and beautiful red-rock formations pierce fields of scrub oak at crazy angles, punched that way by the rising Rocky Mountains eons ago. There are many well-marked trails in the park, one of them leading to the high point, Carpenter Peak.

One day I sat on a boulder at the top of Carpenter Peak geeked-out to the max with my large, full backpack at my side. I sat there with a topographic map and compass trying to pinpoint my exact location. I did this even though I was on a common trail in a popular, well-used park within sight of the Denver skyline and affluent suburban neighborhoods. I got plenty of strange looks and helpful comments that day from patrons carrying only water bottles.

"You are in Roxborough State Park."

"Are you lost?"

"You're at the top of Carpenter Peak."

"Dude, are you homeless?"

I am glad I "located" myself on the map that day in Roxborough State Park: a big "X" on the map where I would bring Kelly one day—for a very important reason.

Sometimes I wonder why it took so long for Kelly and me to meet. I could have saved myself five years of effort and expense. Kelly and I have discussed this, and we both agree that we met at exactly the right time. We both had journeys to complete and things to learn before we were ready to meet each other. We were both the sum of our experiences to that point; they made us who we were. Our relationship works well in this place and time, but would it have five years ago? Ten years ago? Probably not.

We needed to make the journeys we did. Just like I learned how to navigate in the wilderness with a map and compass, I had to learn how to navigate the world of dating and relationships, so I would recognize my destination when I saw it—the right person for me.

Kelly and I have awakened the deepest emotions in each other that we thought were long gone. I know now I needed those five years in the wilderness to learn to appreciate happiness when I found it again. I am so thankful I was blessed with a second chance in life to find that happiness.

My crazy dating experiences using Internet dating services probably seemed like random wanderings to my friends and family. God bless them for being so patient and forbearing.

Not all who wander are lost.

I was just learning how to use a compass.

Chapter 13
Advice I Wish I Had Taken: She Said…

Over the three years I spent meeting people online, I never felt like I became an expert. I continued to learn from dating. I tweaked my profile, updated my pictures, and kept a list of advice I wished I had taken in hopes of not repeating previous mistakes. Here is a portion of that list:

When breaking up, do NOT continue to answer emails. You will not win the argument. You will only keep the fire burning. Don't respond, no matter how much you want to tell him he's an idiot. He will always come back with an equally infuriating, lame, whiny answer, which will only cause you to again wonder what you saw in the guy.

Do not go on a second date with a guy who is on a first name basis with the top ten karaoke DJs in Phoenix. If he wants you to meet him at the restaurant because he needs time to "warm up," don't bother going. He won't even notice you're there.

When asked how a first date went, if your response is, "I'm not sure," you can be reasonably sure you are wasting your time scheduling a second date.

If he doesn't have a car and still has not unpacked fully from a move into a one-bedroom apartment two years ago, this might not be the guy for you.

If his ex-wife is his "best friend," don't bother.

If God as his Savior is mentioned over thirty times in your first phone conversation, chances are he's not going to stop evangelizing long enough to get to know you.

If his list of "must haves" is longer than three pages, you're not it. Skip ahead.

If he's still checking his reflection in the rear view mirror of his jacked-up pickup five minutes after idling in your driveway at the end of the date, jump out. (Look first, it could be a long fall.) Don't glance back. Chances are it will take him another five minutes to notice you're gone.

If all of his previous relationships ended somewhere between blocked emails and a restraining order, RUN, do not walk, to the nearest exit.

If when he finds out you are employed his response is, "Whoa, you might be outta my league!" let this fine catch go.

If he is very specific about how he would like you to be dressed on a first date, he is fixed on turning you into his fantasy mate. Don't make yourself crazy trying to measure up.

If his idea of a great Saturday night date is beer and pizza at your house (you provide the beer and the pizza), and he immediately strips to his boxers upon arrival and turns on ESPN, toss all of the above out the front door and go to Starbucks.

If his first response upon meeting you is, "Boy, honey, you'd make beautiful babies," end the date right there.

If he tends to eat all of his meals at home, lying down…

When his first email conversation starts with, "What are you wearing?" log off. (Actually, it can be fun to mess with this one. You could go into detail about your fuzzy pink bunny slippers, rollers, and green face cream, and then watch how fast he logs off.)

When it's 2007 and he's just discovering email, you might want to move on and let him catch up at his own pace.

If conversation centers on his workout regime, his biceps are more important than you. Move on.

If the word "lackluster" is used more than ten times on your first date, do not be impressed by his big vocabulary. Chances are he is lackluster. Do you want that? No. Move on.

Look for a man with absolutely no potential.

Eric had no potential.

He wasn't potentially a great guy. He was already a great guy.

He didn't have the potential to be kind. He was kind.

He didn't have the potential to have a great job. He already had a great career.

He didn't have the potential to be a wonderful partner. He was.

Eric wasn't a project. I didn't want to change a single thing about him. I was enamored from the start with everything he already was. His lack of potential drew me to him, and it still does today.

Chapter 14
What Colorado Women Want: He Said…

After reading thousands of online profiles of single women in Colorado, I definitely felt a pattern emerge. They all started to sound alike! Let me see if I can recreate a typical one from memory:

ColoradoGal [insert any random number, here]

About Me: I am an attractive, active outdoorswoman who enjoys everything that Colorado has to offer. I am equally comfortable in a pair of blue jeans as I am dressing up for a night on the town. I am scuba certified and travel the world extensively. I have been to France, Mexico, and Germany, and am planning trips to Venezuela, Italy, Norway, New Zealand and just about any other foreign country you can think of. Full disclosure: I have six tattoos.

About You: You must be comfortable in any social situation. I want someone who will treat me like a lady but who is not old fashioned. I want someone without baggage who can travel the world with me. You must be able to make me laugh, and you must love dogs.

Wow.

First, let me congratulate all the world travelers out there. I was a financially struggling single man, supporting a home by myself in an average paying job. I could not afford to join them on all their worldly adventures. I do not know how they do it! Colorado has so much to offer, and there is so much of it I haven't seen. I felt that is where my adventures lay—close to home. Besides, if you can't be where you are, then where are you?

In addition, I am pretty sure you cannot go traveling without "baggage." Actually, I think they meant emotional baggage. That statement always made me laugh. We all have emotional baggage: none of us has led a pain- and disappointment-free life. The key is, do we deal with our disappointments, or do they rule our lives? Or, do we rise above them and move on? Show me a person without baggage, and I will show you someone who has not lived life.

A surprising number of women are scuba certified in Denver. Last time I checked, I found no oceans, here. Just a thought.

I am not a comedian by trade. I am not very good at punchy one-liners. Therefore, I was also very wary of women who made that statement about making them laugh. My humor is based more off my good-natured mannerisms than the jokes of a stand-up comic. I tended to avoid these women, too, because I wanted someone who could make *herself* laugh. Then, I would laugh along with her.

"He must love dogs." I know this is a cliche, and someone made a movie about it. Seriously, though, many women really do say that. Instead, I wanted to meet someone who valued human relationships more than animal ones. I have two cats, and I dated several women who were allergic to them. I never pre-judged anyone on her predisposition to one side of the PetsMart aisle or the other. If I fell madly in love with someone who hated cats, then a compromise would be required; true love should be able to overcome furry complications.

Tongue-in-cheek irony aside, I would like to say that I met many sincere and well-meaning women through online dating. I wish them all the best and hope they have found happiness, too.

Kelly was the first no-compromise person I met with online dating. She was everything I wanted and nothing I didn't. Kelly had two cats of her own. She was almost universally positive and cheerful and made herself, as well as me, laugh often. She felt equally comfortable lounging in blue jeans or dressing up for a night out on the town.

I discovered that online dating really works if you stay true to yourself and remain patient and optimistic. I finally found my ColoradoGal.

Chapter 15
Good Signs/Bad Signs: She Said…

After only about six months in the dating world, I found that there were common signs that told me I was in for a scary date or a good one. Here are a few of the ones I remember:

GOOD SIGNS:

Opens doors

Nice to the waiter

Laughs

Offers to pay (I know this one might offend the feminists, but I found that the courtesy was a sign that my date was considerate. I made sure to offer to return the favor if there was a second date.)

Asks questions

Listens

Smiles

Time flies in his presence

Remembers the little things

The day after our first date I'm still thinking about the cute way he folded his napkin around his coffee mug

Looks at me when he talks

Doesn't take himself or life too seriously

BAD SIGNS:

The first three stories he tells are all depressing

Constantly checks himself out in the mirror

Openly checks out other women in the room

Gives lots of advice (e.g. "You know, what you should do is sell your condo and buy a boat.")

Doesn't listen

Wears more jewelry than I own

Orders a venti, non-fat, mocha with extra whipped cream and an additional shot of espresso at Starbucks, and then he returns it to the Barista because it's "all wrong"

Checks his watch frequently

Takes all incoming cell phone calls during the date

Tends to be an expert at everything

Even though I came to recognize the signs, those big, red flags didn't always deter me from giving a relationship a try. What is it about human nature that makes you want to test it, just to be sure? I was often slow to listen to my instincts. I got better the longer I dated, but politeness and overall optimism sometimes slowed down my intention to run screaming from the room.

On the flip side, when I met Eric I didn't completely trust my instincts either. Everything with him was too easy, too right on the button. I had to eventually drop the doubter in me, relax, and enjoy the reality of a beautiful match.

Chapter 16
One Thing I Have Never Heard Before: He Said…

After five years in the trenches of online dating, I thought I had seen and heard everything. After meeting Kelly and falling crazy in love, I thought I would never have to hear any of it ever again. Then, Kelly told me something I definitely had never heard before.

"Eric, I am an alcoholic."

I'll never forget the night sitting on her couch when she told me this; I can still see the tears streaming down her face. I can't imagine how difficult that was for her, and I feel humbled she possessed the courage to speak up so soon after meeting me. She did not share all of her story with me that night, but I heard enough to know that it didn't matter to me—not in the least.

I like to drink, and I do often. However, I rarely use alcohol as a form of entertainment unto itself and get intoxicated even less often. That's not fun to me; it's scary and dangerous. I thought if anyone could survive living with someone who abstained from alcohol, that person was me. In addition, Kelly assured me that it would not bother her if I drank in her presence. That idea tormented me at first, and the first time I did drink around her, I felt like a most insensitive dork. In the end, though, I felt I had no choice but to honor her trust in me by taking her at her word in this regard.

My tolerance for alcohol is well-defined from my life experiences, and I typically have only a few drinks when we dine out together. This works for us, because I stay sober, too, and we can still enjoy each other's company unclouded by liquor's effects. We have more fun together sober than many people do intoxicated. That rocks…she rocks!

Now that Kelly and I live together, I no longer keep liquor in the house. I made that decision voluntarily. I decided that even though I trust her and she trusts herself, daily temptation such as that would be cruel and could not stand.

I felt sorry about that for a while, and I found myself occasionally wandering around the house looking for my daily gin and tonic, but I got used to it. Alcohol is life and death to her, but it's just booze to me.

Kelly shared more about her disease as time went on. I can't stand the thought of the lonely suffering she experienced; each time I think of it I feel like someone kicked me in the stomach. She cries when she speaks of it. However, instead of fear and pain reflected in her eyes, I see pride and gratitude instead—tears of gratitude. Kelly is the most grateful person I know. She got her life back, and she makes the most of it.

I am so thankful to Alcoholics Anonymous. That organization clearly saved her life. I am awestruck by how people in that program fiercely nurture, love, and support each other through their mutual journeys in health and spirituality. The rest of us in this world could learn from their example.

One day we decided that we had to tell my family about Kelly's alcoholism. In the spirit of loving self-disclosure, we felt we couldn't keep it hidden from them any longer. "Families don't keep secrets from each other," she said. We wanted to tell them on our own terms and avoid any potential awkward situations.

I have never cried more in my life than the day I wrote those emails to my sister and parents, because never before have I felt so much intense pride for someone I loved. I trusted in my family's open-mindedness explicitly; but still, this was not something I ever expected to tell them. I need not have worried, however, for they reacted just the way I expected—with love and open arms.

Kelly will have to attend AA meetings the rest of her life. That is part of the deal—pay it forward—help others to help yourself. I don't regret the time she spends apart from me at those meetings. Life and death—she needs those meetings, and I need her.

If Kelly had a habit of making excuses or deflecting blame away from herself, if she had an escapist personality or a pessimistic attitude toward life, if she felt ashamed instead of being as proud of herself as she is, then her confession that night would have concerned me. Kelly is none of those things—not by a long shot. Kelly applies the lessons she learned in AA to all aspects of her life, and it makes her one of the wisest people I know.

I could not be more impressed, and I'm convinced I could not have pulled myself back from the brink like she did.

You did well, KJ—I love you.

Chapter 17
Broken: She Said…

When I decided to go online to find love, I felt a true mixture of excitement and fear. It was like getting on a roller coaster ride in the dark.

I sat at the computer for one entire evening and filled in my profile to the best of my ability. I tried to be funny, honest, and hopefully intriguing to potential dates. I think I did pretty well, but I definitely didn't get it right the first time. If I were still using Internet dating today, I'm sure I would still be updating and changing my profile.

I was amazed at the sheer number of people who were online, fearlessly putting themselves out there in search of a match. I was thrilled at the opportunity to meet some of them, and I just knew the right guy was out there…somewhere. Seeing all of those pictures and tag lines pop up the first time I logged on made me hopeful and a little giddy at the possibilities before me.

It was kind of amusing how my perspective changed a year or so later. I found out the hard way that not everyone out there is trying to meet their soul mate. Some are just looking for a mate for a date, and that was their prerogative. I found that it was pretty important to be up-front about the fact that I was ultimately looking for a lasting relationship. It saved a lot of awkward missed signals later on.

I eventually started to see former dates pop on and off. If they were gone for a while, I assumed they must be in a new relationship. Then, I would see their profile appear again. I was slightly sorry that something must not have worked out as they hoped. I know I had the same pattern.

I developed sort of a "cast a wide net" technique. I would select several guys who seemed promising, venture out on a bunch of first dates, and usually out of those first dates I would meet someone interesting. We generally dated for around three months (three months was the magic number between moving into a serious relationship and the knowledge that it wasn't going anywhere), and then I would be back online meeting a whole new slew of possibilities.

I learned a few things the hard way. I eventually played down the fact that I had been an actor and a singer, because it tended to attract men who thought they would be dating a supermodel or something. I can sing really well, but I'm not Cindy Crawford.

I was told in my first actual relationship (lasting about three months) that I was "low maintenance" as a girlfriend. I assumed that was a compliment. So, I decided to add it to my profile after we decided to call it quits. That wasn't a bright idea, either. The universal response was, "If you have to say you're low maintenance, either you really aren't, or you're a doormat."

I also found out that loading a fun picture of skiing in Breckenridge was not necessarily a great idea. Evidently, my parka, hat, gloves, and sunglasses didn't offer any opportunity for the prospective dates to get a good look at me. A less-than-polite first date gave me a hard time about including a picture that pretty much gave him a glimpse of my nose. At the time I was annoyed. I knew for sure I wouldn't be putting a swimsuit picture on there anytime soon. But after I learned to listen and find the kernel of truth in what he was saying, I realized he had a point.

It was hard for me at first to talk about myself. I felt like the profile was asking me to brag, and it felt pretty uncomfortable. After many revisions and numerous first dates, my profile gradually became more specific as I saw what responses came from the words I chose.

Did I care if my date was religious? I found out that as much as I think everyone has a right to his own spiritual path, it was pretty important to me that the guy was at least on one.

Was education important? I wanted to say that it wasn't. I wanted to be an equal opportunity dater. In truth, I just got along better with guys who shared a similar educational background. We tended to speak a more similar language.

What about family background? Without question, I was more attracted to men who had a positive relationship with their parents and most or all of their siblings.

My profile went through countless revisions. However, it was through face-to-face contact that I really learned what mattered.

I remember having dinner with a very nice gentleman one evening. He was smart, funny, tall, good-looking, kind—he seemed to have it all. We talked a little about our jobs, our backgrounds, about previous relationships, and then he threw me for a loop.

He said that all of us using Internet dating were "broken" people. We had all failed at relationships, and we were looking to pick up the pieces with each other.

I stared at him and pretended to continue to listen to his theory, but that's when I knew he wasn't the guy for me. What kept running through my mind was, *I'm not broken.*

Even at the darkest moments in my life, I am still a viable, significant, loved human being. My failures and setbacks are the things that have molded me into the person I am today. I wanted to challenge the man to show me a person who hasn't had disappointments or failures in life.

Internet dating is not the Island of Misfit Toys! It's a place for people who are single to meet each other. It's as simple as that. I didn't go to bars anymore, and I never had the nerve to flirt with someone in the grocery store. At the gym I'm a sweaty mess, so that wasn't the best place to pick up guys. Online, I could get to know a little more about a person before we went out. He was not a random guy I ran across in the parking lot or something (not ran into, ran across).

There was another bonus to putting my thoughts and priorities into words for my profile's narrative. I found out a lot more about myself when I had to spell out what makes me tick and what is important to me in a relationship.

When I met Eric online, I knew from his profile that we shared something very important. We shared a passion for life. We were not broken individuals. We were strong, capable, fallible, caring, sometimes silly people who experienced life to the fullest.

It took awhile for me to find my true match, but the journey was part of the discovery. Eric was worth the wait.

Chapter 18
Another Thing I Have Never Heard Before: He Said…

An upright Shimmel piano stands in a recessed nook of our dining room. The black surface of the instrument shines with a lacquered perfection marred only by occasional cat footprints. The elegant, ebony surface reminds me of the elegant woman who owns it, and to me symbolizes her life before we met. Kelly is a professional-caliber singer.

I heard the stories, saw the newspaper clippings, and wondered what her life was like back then: the New England Conservatory, New York City, Broadway tours, and regional theatres. I saw a stunning picture of Kelly on stage once, in costume; a moment in time captured with her arm extended toward the audience, her lips parted for a note that has long since fallen silent. I know in my heart that the woman in the picture is Kelly—I recognize her—but my mind has trouble believing the larger-than-life, powerful image of beauty in the photograph is the same sweet, adorable woman at my side.

Believe it, Eric. The picture is of her, and she is wearing the ring you gave her on her finger.

When I heard Kelly sing in church for the first time, I swore all the lights in the sanctuary must have been illuminating her face. You can't help but pick her bright expression and radiant face out from a crowd, instantly. Her father was with me in the congregation that night. When the performance ended, he turned to me and said with a sly smile, "That was nothing."

"Nothing?" I sniffled, wiping away tears of pride from my cheeks. How could that divine performance have been nothing?

"Just wait 'til she really goes for it, someday," he said.

I think there comes a moment in every true relationship for a man when the woman he loves does something so endearing that he knows he made the right choice. He knows it in his heart, and the feeling captures his soul forever.

For me, that moment came when Kelly sat at her piano and sang for me for the first time. She sang "Round Midnight" by Thelonious Monk. I could hear hints of her powerful voice in the intentionally subdued, ephemeral way she sang the haunting piece, and I believed. I believed that no one else could have touched me the way she did with her voice that night. I stood behind her and watched her face reflected in the shiny, black surface of the piano as she sang. I like standing behind her when she is at the piano. I can gaze at her reflection without her knowledge and soak in the soothing music—beauty, grace…elegance.

I finally experienced the full extent of Kelly's gift on an evening she warmed up before a choir audition at a new church we were attending. Her voice filled the house with a power that rooted me to the kitchen floor. I froze in place, paused in mid-motion, unable to move. This was definitely something I had never heard before. Kelly's cats scattered for cover, but mine, always curious, sat at the foot of the piano, as entranced as I was.

The clear, bright tone of Kelly's voice enters the walls and floors of our home like a living presence and its energy travels up through your legs, rivets you where you stand, and resonates deep in your gut.

That's power.

That's my baby.

Chapter 19
00733: She Said…

When I first met Eric, one of the most intriguing things he told me about himself was that he was training to be part of a search-and-rescue team. I wasn't entirely sure what that meant, so I followed up with a few more questions. He was very modest in his explanation, and I only found out after we moved in together exactly what his volunteer job entailed. I remember on that first date in Starbucks, though, a little light bulb went off.

Hmmm, he volunteers, I thought. *That means he does things for other people…on purpose…without getting paid. One big gold star for this guy.*

I have to admit, my mind wandered a little at that point. I have no idea what he talked about next. I was imagining him running off to find poor, stranded, starving, injured hikers in the mountains. It was easy to picture the handsome man sitting across from me decked out in what I imagined to be some sort of modified fireman's outfit, bounding off into the wilderness, braving the snow and cold to save the day. I was smitten.

A few weeks later, I was lucky enough to catch a glimpse of a picture someone on the team emailed Eric after a recent training. There he was, my hero, hanging off a CLIFF, dangling from a rope with his feet planted against the vertical rock, looking all muscle-y and tough. My heart melted. Was I dating James Bond? Or was he Dudley Do-Right? The skeptic that was still living in my head at the time thought, this was way too good to be true.

By the way, the rest of that picture was revealed to me months later. The cliff he and his fellow trainees were dangling from left them poised a full three feet from the safety of earth. Not quite as death-defying as I first imagined, but he still looked really cool all geared up.

I finally got a taste of the real thing a couple weeks after we moved in together. I was brushing my teeth, and Eric was walking around the downstairs turning off lights and getting ready to call it a night, too. Then, all hell broke loose.

Alarms went off (his beeper—several times in a row), cats went scurrying everywhere, and in a bright yellow flash, Eric was on his way out the door. All I could do was hand him a couple of protein bars and give him a quick kiss goodbye. I stood stunned in the hallway with all four cats lined up in front of me like a drill team, staring at the front door, listening to his Jeep back out of the garage. I felt lonely and proud at the same time.

He returned at two in the morning, tired and dirty, but grinning from ear to ear. Obviously, this was his calling. I asked him about the mission, and he excitedly told me about trudging through the mud on the banks of a river, looking for a possible drowning victim. Does that sound like fun, or what?

Eric's radio number is 733, so I have taken to calling him Double-O-733, which I'm pretty sure embarrasses the heck out of him. He is my James Bond—running off whenever his beeper sounds the alarm, with a backpack full of ropes and gadgets that mystify me.

Eric's spirit of compassion and his desire to help those in need is something that drew me to him. He is not boastful, and he sure doesn't pick easy volunteer jobs. I hand out slices of pizza to kids at a teen center as a volunteer. My hero throws on snowshoes and a forty-pound backpack to search for a missing person. His mind is on the families of the lost and how he would feel if he were in their shoes. I love him, because he lives his life with such passion and joy. I love him, because he wants to be there to help when people need it the most. I love him, well, just because.

He fulfills my fantasies with his search-and-rescue work, but more importantly, he contributes in a meaningful way to his community. He helps people. He offers his talents, and he expects nothing in return. Eric is my hero.

Chapter 20
One More Try: He Said…

After five years of trying to find a lasting relationship on the Web, my patience and motivation were running thin. I had a hard time telling a first date I had been online for so long. That embarrassed me for a while, as if I were broken and incapable of finding a lasting relationship. On the other hand, maybe it gave the impression I was too choosy and too quick to reject potential mates. Who knows?

Comparing notes from the trenches with a first date is an easy way to break the ice. "How long have you been Internet dating? Do you like the experience? Have you met any nice people?" It's hard to avoid the question.

Sometimes I would be vague and say, "A few years." Other times I would simply say, "Long enough." If I was feeling brave I would say "Five years," cringe, and wait for the inevitable look of pity from across the table. The real answer, I decided, was that a love worth finding was a love worth waiting for. Once I realized this, I answered the question truthfully, with no apologies.

The paradox of my life in those later days fascinated me. I finally felt I had come close to arriving as a well-rounded person outside the dating scene. Hobbies, volunteerism, and professional and personal growth activities were in full swing. On the other hand, the compulsion to "fix" my singleness by finding someone remained intense, and I had to guard constantly from allowing that compulsion to rule my life.

Despite the years of disappointments, I did a good job of maintaining my optimism that this online system could work. I went in to each first date asking, "Why not?" I took the attitude that each person could potentially be the "one," and acted like it. I think women appreciated my optimism and appreciated the fact that I was not just another gloomy Gus who complained about other women while not finding success in romance. However, as time wore on, it became harder and harder for me to maintain that optimism, and I took longer to rebound between disappointments.

During the last year, I turned my profile on and off numerous times. I thought I had the strength to say I was okay as a single person, and I didn't need to be trying so hard to find a match and investing all that time, money, and mental energy. Each time, though, I would turn my profile back on after a couple of weeks and dive back in. It was kind of like an addiction I could not break. "Just one more try!"

A couple of relationships near the end affected me greatly and caused me to seriously consider giving up the online dating experiment for good.

One woman and I spent nearly every minute of a three-day holiday weekend together. I could tell she felt emotionally invested, and I thought I was, too. Then, at an evening meal the third day, I had an overwhelming realization that this person was not right for me. I had a terrible, sinking feeling in my stomach, and I wanted to just slide off my seat and disappear.

While driving home, I canceled our remaining evening plans and told her I needed some time alone. She must have read the writing on the wall, for I heard the pain in her voice as she told me it was okay for me to drive her home. I hated myself; I was tired of messing with people's lives. That's not who I am.

Another relationship that lowered my self-esteem was with an attractive woman who took me for a ride. We made first email contact in the morning. By noon, we were having lunch; by evening, we were snuggling at the movie theatre. She told me she had just left a long-term relationship. I should have seen that as a serious red flag. Even after five years of dating people in the online world, I had trouble seeing the red flags coming. After a three-day whirlwind of romance and fun, she dropped me as quickly as she found me, for no apparent reason and without explanation. I was equally tired of people messing with me—and adding red flags to my collection.

That was pretty much the breaking point. I knew in my heart I either had to put my money where my mouth was and live the happy and whole life I knew I could as a single person, or stay trapped in the dating cycle forever. Even then—*even then*—I left my profile online. Thank God I did.

One more try.

kjo2snow just winked at you. Out of millions of members, she picked you! Flirt back right away with a wink, or even better, an intriguing email.

Okay!

Chapter 21
One More Time: She Said…

At the conclusion of my Valentine's Day date from hell I was ready to call it quits, or at least take a break from dating. I sat on the couch, stuffing my face with chocolate and glaring at the beautiful couples embracing on the Soap Network. I wondered if I had spent the last three years making a complete fool of myself, thinking I would find my perfect match in the sea of faces online.

After a five-minute pity party, I looked around and took in my surroundings. I lived in a beautiful home. I had a great job. I loved my family. I was sober. I had a crew of awesome friends. I enjoyed a full schedule of volunteer activities, singing in church, visiting family up in the mountains…. I was in charge of my daily activities, and I didn't have to answer to anyone.

I decided right then that I had a great life. I didn't need a man to complete it. Dating was fun, but if I ended up "single lady with cats," that was just fine with me. I popped another chocolate into my mouth and smiled at Yin and Yang, who were curled up on either side of me. Life was good.

A few days later, I logged on and half-heartedly scanned the profiles while I ate a late dinner. I figured I might find a date for the weekend, but I no longer had any aspirations to discover Mr. Wonderful.

That's when I saw Eric's profile.

A friend of mine told me a year before that I would probably run into my Prince Charming when I gave up. Huh. There he was.

Who is this Kyle guy? I thought. (His online name was KyletheCat.) *Where has he been? I don't remember him. Hey! He's handsome—and tall. He's kinda funny, too. Aw, look at the picture of him with… oh, please don't be his daughter, please, please… his niece! That's sweet.*

I think I winked at him first. I was bolder after I stopped searching for Mr. Right. Anyhow, we struck up a conversation, and the rest is history.

We had to wait a couple of days for our first date, because he had a previous commitment. I cringed as the little skeptic in my head said, *He's probably stringing along several ladies…or he's married or something, because this guy is too good to be true.*

Skeptic dude was wrong. Eric was scheduled to have dinner with his sister, brother-in-law, niece, and nephew. He honored family commitments and wasn't about to change them for some chick he just met.

He actually emailed me when he returned home that night and informed me that he spent part of the evening decked out in a tiara and earrings. I thought it was a tad early to be telling me about his cross-dressing habits, but it turns out he was playing "Pretty Princess" with his niece. Now, THAT is a guy who is confident in his masculinity. Not everyone looks good in a tiara.

Eric and I very rarely spoke on the phone the first few days we corresponded. For some reason it was awkward. It still is, and that is really funny to me. I can jabber on to my parents or my girlfriends for hours. (My dad likes to give me a hard time about it. "She's talking, and she can't shut up.") But with Eric, it's different. We prefer taking the time to craft love notes and email them to each other throughout the day. I think we've sent thousands of them so far. Eric and I talk nonstop face to face (when we're not kissing). We're just not phone talkers, and that's fine.

Another friend of mine had suggested three years previously that I make a list of the traits of my perfect match. I did so, grudgingly at the time, and I assumed the guy my list portrayed did not exist in the real world. After Eric and I had been corresponding only one day, I pulled out my list, which was hidden between two books in the guest room closet. Wow. It just might be him.

The day of our first date finally came, and my stomach did flip-flops all the way from my car to the entrance of Starbucks. There was an extremely handsome sandy-haired gentleman in a bright red shirt sitting casually near the entrance. *Oh please, please, please, let that be him.* He stood and smiled, looking me directly in the eyes. "Hi, I'm Eric."

I don't remember a whole lot from that first date. I know he bought the coffee. I remember being taken aback by the way he gazed directly into my eyes, like we'd known each other for years. I remember losing my concentration when I fantasized a little about his search-and-rescue gig. Then, my mind skips to our departure in the parking lot. He moved in for what I thought was a goodbye kiss on the cheek, but instead his lips just grazed mine and sent lightning bolts through my entire body.

I wanted to look up to heaven and say, "All RIGHT, God. I get it. This is him. You don't have to hit me over the head. Geez."

On my way home, I called my parents, and as usual, they were full of questions.

"Soooo, how was your date?" they prodded, always optimistic.

"Fine."

I was afraid to let the cat out of the bag, so to speak.

Chapter 22
3,454 Emails: He Said…

Users of the online dating system I used can indicate interest in another person without composing an email by "winking" at that person. This is a low-risk, one-click way to take the first step.

Some people appreciated winks, while others did not. I went either way. Sometimes I would respond to winks, other times I ignored them. Sometimes I would use them to let a woman know I was interested, but for the most part, I tried to make the effort to send personalized emails to each individual. Sometimes, though, when I got frustrated, I would wink at twenty or thirty people at once, sit back, and wait for the influx of emails from interested women to come pouring in.

That never happened.

One snowy February weekend, however, I received a system message telling me *kjo2snow* had winked at me. I liked *kjo2snow's* profile: she seemed like a modest, genuine person, and she had a couple of nice pictures of herself posted. I responded to her wink by thanking her and inviting her to write back and tell me more about herself. Her emails were endearing—positive, cheerful notes. She wrote in complete sentences with proper punctuation. That was huge to me—it indicated intelligence, education, and organized thinking. I usually declined to meet people who could not write.

I learned that her name was Kelly, and that she claimed Iowa as her home state. Iowa! What a relief! I usually found I got along with fellow Midwesterners best. There seems to be something about a common upbringing—a common frame of societal reference—that has a strong, positive influence on how relationships work. I'm from Iowa, too. (No, I am not a farm boy.)

I visited my sister's family that first day of emails, and played with my then three-year-old niece after dinner. Somehow, we ended up playing "Pretty

Princess" together. My niece can play "Pretty Princess" like no other girl can, but I hate to lose. Soon, I was wearing all the jewelry. Ha! Take that! Of course, I had to write Kelly about it as soon as I got home.

I had a good time at my sister's tonight. I somehow got roped into playing Pretty Princess with my 3 y.o. niece. So, imagine me wearing earrings, necklace, and a tiara. (If you want to stop emailing me now and run away screaming, I would understand completely.) I have to return for babysitting duty this Friday. Maybe we can watch Dora the Explorer on TV that night, instead. Oh! What am I saying!!!!! D'oh!

The next morning I had deep regrets. Now she'll think I'm a women's-jewelry-wearing cross-dresser. She thought it was cute, however. Phew, dodged one bullet!

Several enjoyable emails later, I had a good feeling about Kelly and suggested a meeting. The longer I used Internet dating, the more impatient I became with the emailing preamble phase of introductions. I got tired of wasting my time, if nothing was to become of it. Sometimes, I would cut straight to the heart of the matter: "Hi-my-name-is-Eric-want-to-meet-over-coffee?"

I applied the Rule of Starbucks Proximity to Kelly. Thus, exactly halfway between our homes, on a straight line, there was an open-air mall called Aspen Grove with a Starbucks. Of course! We met that evening, barely twenty-four hours after that first "wink."

Kelly's online pictures did not prepare me adequately for how striking she is in person. I arrived at Starbucks first and sat in a chair near the door, watching people come and go. Finally, a tall, elegant, dark-haired woman appeared to be heading my way. Oh-please, oh-please, oh-please: "Hi, I'm Kelly!" she said.

I don't remember much about that first meeting at Starbucks. I must have paid the cashier, must have picked up the coffee from the Barista without spilling; we must have found a free table somehow. I know we had a nice, long talk. My mind always fast-forwards to our goodbye in the parking lot and that age-old dilemma: hug, kiss or handshake? Lips or cheek?

I gave Kelly the slightest, softest kiss on the lips I could manage as I said goodbye. I probably ruined everything with the kiss. That was way too forward! Rats!

Kelly appreciated the kiss—dodged another bullet—and all the kisses to follow. I felt like we were on to something, but in light of all my recent disappointments, I kept my emotions in check. Wow! She liked my Jeep, and she liked my two cats; she had two of her own. She didn't have any kids and didn't want any. (Yay!) Things were looking up.

I invited her to dinner at my house a couple of nights later for a home-cooked meal. I must have really liked her; for I seemed eager to convince her I was "normal." (I guess she had a history with some guy with a piano?) I sent her this email to apologize in advance for my quirky foibles.

...there are a few things you need to know about my house first. These issues may be construed as a slight departure from normalcy—we'll see what you think. I have a treadmill in my dining room. I have a floor project that has gone unfinished for two years. My garage entry door has duct tape over the missing knob. And, I am currently storing the back seat to my Jeep in the front entry way. I hope these items have not scared you away. At least I am not a piano murderer, right?

A few weeks ago, Kelly showed me her *Google* calendar, where she recorded all of our dates the first few weeks. What a full schedule of romantic adventures! It was fun to see proof a year later of how much fun we really did have in those early days and continue to have to this day.

I finally allowed myself to believe we were on to something. Okay! DO NOT TELL YOUR MOTHER. No bad karma allowed.

Another thing I appreciated about Kelly is that she was not much of a phone conversationalist. We barely spoke on the phone at all. I'm not either, and I felt most uncomfortable with women who kept me on the phone for hours. I think we spoke by phone maybe three times the first few months. We shared hundreds of emails during that time, though. That tradition continues to this day, and I think we are up to 3,000 or 4,000 messages by now. I wrote this one after a particularly absent-minded morning of daydreaming about Kelly.

I should be able to get lots of work done today. I'm not distracted at all. That making tea with hot coffee thing could have happened to anyone. And, who hasn't put a box of Triscuits in the fridge from time to time? Locking the cat in a closet? He must have deserved it. Finally, driving to work and leaving the garage door up? Clearly, that wasn't my fault. See, what I mean? Nope, no distractions today.

I think I knew Kelly was my perfect match when we watched the Academy Awards together a week after our first meeting. We contrived a good-natured competition where we predicted the winners in each category. Whoever guessed the award correctly received a kiss from the other.

Since neither of us had actually seen any of the movies up for awards that year, it was mostly a crapshoot, so we gave up and started kissing after each announcement, anyway. I thought that was the most romantic thing ever, and we laughed and kissed all night. Someone who could make a silly, fun, romantic game like that for the longest, most boring TV awards show had to be the gal for me. I knew I was in love.

My birthday was only two weeks away—I had to get busy!

Chapter 23
Attack of the Killer Grape Tomatoes: We Said…

She said:

The first two weeks we dated were filled with laughter. They were highly electric and super romantic…but mostly they were filled with lots and lots of laughter.

One perfect example is a dinner we planned together, where I would meet two of Eric's close friends for the first time. My job was to bring "salad fixings," which would not be a big deal to the average person, but I should mention here that I have absolutely no aptitude for anything that goes on in a kitchen. My family members have had a lot of fun with this fact over the years. My hockey puck cookies are legendary. Four years ago, my mom and dad bought me a set of kitchen towels that have a beautifully embroidered phrase on them, "*Last time I cooked, hardly anyone got sick.*"

Needless to say, I had no idea what to bring, other than lettuce. I wanted to give his friends a good first impression, so I decided Costco would have everything I needed. I wandered aimlessly through the vegetable section, feeling very awkward and completely at a loss. Finally, I picked out a fancy looking tub of mixed greens, croutons, and a vat of grape tomatoes. (They looked cute.)

The evening started off very well. Eric's friends were wonderful and put me at ease immediately by telling embarrassing stories about Eric. We wanted the evening to be stress-free, so we threw a pre-made pan of lasagna into the oven and started to assemble the salad.

I pulled my ingredients out of the bag, and Eric's eyes popped out of his head when he saw my tub o' tomatoes. Evidently, I went a little overboard. Unfortunately, their sheer numbers drew the attention of everyone, and I found out pretty quickly that no one liked grape tomatoes except for Eric. He couldn't stop laughing at the fact that I bought enough of the little red buggers to feed the Denver Rescue Mission, and I don't even like tomatoes.

That's not the best part. My favorite part of this story is what Eric did next.

He said:

I have never seen such a large container of grape tomatoes. It was like the size of a shoebox, or something. It was scary. Who would buy such a thing? Someone who loved tomatoes, I thought.

When dinner was served, I put a few tomatoes on my salad, and then passed around the toolbox-sized container. Both of my guests refused. That's okay. That was their prerogative. I was sure Kelly would take some, though—she bought them, after all. She didn't. "Why?" I asked.

"I don't like tomatoes," she said.

I sputtered and stammered. "Are you kidding me? You bought all these, and you don't even like them? I can't eat all these myself!"

The four of us had a long, hard laugh about that, and dinner continued. We had an enjoyable evening of food and fellowship that night with the other couple. I was so pleased to introduce Kelly to them and hoped it was the beginning of a long friendship among the four of us.

"What was the deal with the grape tomatoes?" I asked Kelly later that evening when we had the house to ourselves again. "Why did you bring them if you don't even like to eat them?"

"You told me to bring fixings for a salad."

"But why so many?" I asked.

"They looked cute."

I was incredulous. "Did they speak to you, too?"

"Maybe."

I don't think I've ever laughed as hard as Kelly and I did that night. That's one thing I love about us, we laugh about the most random, little things. Silliness is a way of life with us. The laugh lines on my face have doubled since we met. I can live with that. Every day for weeks, I had to tease Kelly about the tomato incident.

The massive, ice-chest-sized box of grape tomatoes stayed in my refrigerator for several weeks. It was an impossible quantity for one person to eat.

She said:

Did I mention Eric has an endearing tendency to exaggerate?

He said:

Hey! *I'm* telling this story…

Anyway, I saw that the tomatoes were finally starting to go bad, so I had to throw them away. Wait! I had a sneaky plan.

I am an early bird; well…I am a night owl, too. Okay, I'm an insomniac. Anyway, I was up early one morning and decided I would play a joke on Kelly Jo. I took out the foot-locker-sized box of grape tomatoes and arranged them in a line leaving the refrigerator, down and around the kitchen floor.

They looked like an army of red, bloated ants; I left the fridge door ajar, as if the tomato army was making an escape. I snapped a picture of this and emailed it to Kelly with the title "Help Me! The Tomatoes Are Escaping!"

She thought it was very funny. Hilarious.

I guess you had to be there.

Chapter 24
Happy Birthday to Me: She Said…

My fiance is sneaky. It's one of the things that I love about him. He's not creepy sneaky. He doesn't lurk around in the shadows or anything…as far as I know. He's good sneaky.

Eric is a true romantic.

We met on February 19th, and by February 20th I was fighting off the bells in my head announcing, *This is THE guy! Right here! Stop looking! This is the one! Rejoice!*

Those bells were admittedly drowned out by the ugly little cynic who had taken up residence in my head a few months prior to when we met—the one who was just waiting to find out that this was too good to be true. My cynic disappeared within the first week, and I'm happy to say the voices in my head are mostly merry these days.

Back to the sneaky thing—he proposed to me on HIS birthday! Can you believe it? How on earth would a jaded divorcee who had been meeting men online for close to three years ever have seen that coming? THAT is sneaky.

It took me a long time to pick out a birthday present for Eric. I was so in love with the guy, I couldn't see straight. Nevertheless, we had only known each other three weeks. What could I get him that would show I put some thought into the gift, but not give away the fact that I was hopelessly gaga over him? Was there a middle ground somewhere? I went with a package of several items which had meaning to the two of us, but probably wouldn't send him running for the nearest exit.

The plan was for him to pick me up early in the morning so we could be the first ones on the trail at Roxborough Park. I smiled when my alarm went off that morning.

I hopped out of bed, sending my two kittens, Yin and Yang, tumbling across the covers. This man was going to turn me into a morning person. Who wouldn't want to become a morning person if it meant spending a few more hours looking up into his handsome blue eyes?

The day was not only Eric's birthday, but it was our first hiking excursion together, and I was a little nervous. I knew Eric was part of some hiking club, and he was in training for search-and-rescue. I had seen his backpack, and I couldn't lift it. My experience with hiking in Arizona had been a T-shirt, a pair of shorts, sneakers with big treads, and a water bottle. I didn't even own a backpack. The day before our date, I ran to REI to get long winter underwear and a hat. That was a start. Maybe Eric (my hero) would want to teach me the rest. I decided not to pretend I knew what I was doing. Just be honest and learn something. I knew I wouldn't fool him into thinking I had the background of a park ranger.

As I struggled into my long johns that morning, my head was still in the clouds from our romantic dinner the night before. Images of holding hands and smiling and whispering in a secluded booth danced in my groggy thoughts. Eric kept playing with my fingers at the table after dinner, and I thought it was sweet how he looked at my hands so intently. (I was also relieved I had recently gotten a manicure.) I couldn't remember what I ate. I couldn't remember our waitress. I couldn't even remember how we got to the restaurant. I did remember thinking, *I can't believe I'm here with this guy! I'm so lucky.*

Sparks flew between us all night. The energy was palpable to the point where I felt that we were the light source for the entire restaurant. It had been torture saying goodbye to him late that evening. The only consolation was that I would see him again in a few short hours.

The doorbell rang at exactly seven-thirty. I wondered—not for the first time—if he sat outside my door waiting for the clock to reach our agreed-upon appointment. Eric was never late. That was a habit I could learn from him, too.

We were the first to arrive at the trail, and all of my misgivings about being inadequately prepared for the hike melted away. I was in the capable, strong hands of my hero. He knew where to go, what to bring, how long it would take, where the best views would be. He took care of everything. I would have followed him anywhere.

About a half hour later, we stared at majestic red rocks jutting out of the smooth landscape from a lookout spot halfway through the hike. I wondered if I had ever before been so happy, sharing the beauty of God's creation with the man I loved. Then, that sneaky boy threw me over the edge.

Not literally! He didn't throw me over the cliff.

Eric declared his love for me, and I realized only partway through his speech that he was proposing. I have no idea what he said to me after that moment of realization. Bells were ringing again in my head.

I must have looked pretty stunned, because he had to ask me if I wanted to see the ring. We both took a giant step away from the ledge before he reached into his pocket and pulled out the most beautiful ring I have ever seen. How did he know that I wear mostly silver jewelry? How did he guess my exact ring size? I don't even know my ring size.

I have never been so surprised in my entire life, and I have never been so completely sure of my answer. "Yes, yes, my answer is yes," I kept repeating, as we held each other close on that bright March morning. When we finally released our embrace, we found that we were surrounded by a small herd of deer. Our group of witnesses looked at us approvingly, then gracefully and silently stepped through the trees, leaving us alone again.

The rest of the hike was jubilant, and by the time we returned to Eric's Jeep, we realized we would soon be facing one serious issue. My family knew next to nothing about Eric, and his family knew next to nothing about me. This would be interesting.

"Is this the guy from Colorado Springs?"

"No, Dad."

"The swim coach?"

"No, Mom. That was a few months ago."

"What's his name?"

"Eric."

"Well, that's great! I hope it works out."

Happy birthday…to me.

Chapter 25
Happy Birthday to Me: He Said…

Being sneaky is cool. I like doing the unexpected; cliches are no fun, especially when it comes to love and romance. I knew I was going to propose to Kelly by about week two of dating her. The only two issues were when and how. Sneaky.

We met on February 19, and my thirty-eighth birthday was on March 11. What could be sneakier than proposing on *my* birthday? I knew she would never suspect a thing, but could I pull it off in time?

I am not that observant, but I did notice that the only wristwatch I ever saw her wear was silver. Did that mean she favored silver jewelry? That was slim evidence, at best. No problem, the ring must be silver. What size, though? I knew I could not ask her that. The operation had to be a complete surprise, so I could not ask any of her friends or family, either. That was fine, because I had not yet met them.

We would just have to travel to the jewelers immediately to resize the ring, if she accepted. Not ideal, but I could live with it. Where could I pop the question? What location could provide an appropriate backdrop? Of course—Roxborough State Park, my favorite place. No cliches allowed.

My criteria at the jewelry store were simple: silver, simple, and elegant. I made a surprisingly swift circuit of the glass cases in showroom floor, leaving the salesperson slack-jawed in my wake. I knew exactly what I wanted.

Unfortunately, however, I made the wrong choice.

I had a sense of foreboding that I had made a less-than-ideal selection, so I returned to the store the following day. I saw the band I had identified as choice number two still in the case and decided that was the one for Kelly. "What size would you like it?" the salesperson asked.

"I don't know, and I don't care," I replied, and I put the ring on layaway that day.

I returned on the third day to pay the balance due—so much for layaway. I had a fleeting thought that shopping for an engagement ring two weeks after meeting someone was crazy, but this was Kelly—no problem.

Kelly and I shared an incredibly romantic dinner the night before my birthday at a restaurant we would later choose as our wedding reception location. I don't know if she remembers this or not, but I kept playing with her fingers and staring at them, as I held her soft hands. Would the ring fit?

The morning of Sunday, March 11, arrived clear and sunny, a perfect day for a late winter hike. Unusually heavy snowfall had buried metro Denver that winter, so we felt blessed to get outdoors; it felt like spring. We arrived at the park just at opening time—I wanted privacy most of all, and ours was the first car in the parking lot.

The Fountain Valley Trail leaves the visitor center and makes a loop down to an old homestead house and back. Along the way, the Lyons Overlook trail cuts through thick scrub oak and leads to a wooden deck overlooking the park's famous red rock formations. These red rocks, similar to the ones found at Red Rocks Amphitheater in Morrison and Garden of the Gods in Colorado Springs, form one of the more distinctive scenic places in Colorado's Front Range.

We stood there on the observation deck holding hands and soaking in the sights of the silent, sentinel rocks surrounding us. Then, I knew the time had come. I pulled the box out of my pocket, but had the most horrid, panicked thought. What would happen if I dropped the ring off the cliff? *Tink, tink, ta-tink, ta-tink... tink... tink.*

With the imagined sound of metal on rock still ringing in my ears, I opened the box and made my speech, standing well away from the edge. Unfortunately, I blanked out and don't remember a thing I said. Whatever it was, she must have approved, for she allowed me to slip the ring on her finger.

It slid on perfectly. Straight from the jeweler's case, the ring fit perfectly—no rushed trip to the store for re-sizing required.

I still do not know Kelly's ring size. I'm not sure if she does, either.

We embraced and talked softly for several minutes together, flushed with excitement and joy, and then we looked up. A herd of a dozen or so small deer had surrounded us up on the plateau, silently grazing the vegetation in the scrub oak that circled us. We looked on in amazement at these silent witnesses to our precious moment; they continued to graze, eventually moving on and down the slope. We felt honored to have them there with us, as if they blessed our decision with their presence.

The remainder of the hike was joyful and giddy. I enjoyed hearing her reaction to my gift and was gratified to know she was completely surprised. We hadn't even used the "marriage" word with each other until that day. That ring was the first gift I had ever given Kelly. Sneaky.

Kelly teased me afterward that the day could have turned into my worst birthday ever, had she declined. I had never thought of that possibility. I had felt strangely confident and calm about the whole thing. It turned out to be my best birthday, and now the last remaining task in my sneaky plan was to tell our families.

"Kelly who?"

Chapter 26
In Summary: We Said…

Looking back over our separate histories, it seems obvious to us that we were two magnets making our way through a forest of humanity toward each other. As much as we cherish every moment together today and sometimes wish we could have met sooner, we could not have sped up the process. The path was just as important as the destination.

We have learned so much…so far. Now we get to start on a new road together. We wake up each morning with joy and expectancy.

What are we in for today?

Thanks, God, for allowing us to do this together.

Here are just a few of the things we have discovered along the way:

Never give up hope.

Be comfortable in your own skin first.

Don't try to be what someone else wants.

Be authentic to yourself.

Laugh often.

Make the most of second chances.

Don't be mean. It just puts bad karma out there.

Never, ever admit defeat.

Do something for someone else. It releases you from self-pity, and it feels great!

No matter what your past mistakes, you deserve *happiness* today.

First dates come and go, but family is forever.

You can never have too many cats.

When people ask us how we met, we still grin from ear to ear, because we know that we are incredibly lucky to have found each other…or maybe we were destined to meet. Who knows? It's a hard question to answer, but we are bursting at the seams to share our happiness.

We met at Starbucks. That's the short answer.

Chapter 27
The Final Tally

546 First dates
293 Second dates
105 Third dates
1 Match!
2 People
4 Cats
2 Houses
1 Home
2 Cars
0 Cars
1 Jeep
2 Jeeps
5,453 Emails
3 Phone calls
2 Million grape tomatoes
1 Love that will last a lifetime

CPSIA information can be obtained at www.ICGtesting.com
Printed in the USA
BVOW020105040412

286816BV00001B/13/P

9 781605 631639